Jump In!

By Vanessa Reilly

A

OXFORD

UNIVERSITY PRESS

OXFORD
UNIVERSITY PRESS

Great Clarendon Street, Oxford, OX2 6DP, United Kingdom

Oxford University Press is a department of the University of Oxford.
It furthers the University's objective of excellence in research, scholarship,
and education by publishing worldwide. Oxford is a registered trade
mark of Oxford University Press in the UK and in certain other countries

CLASS BOOK PACK ISBN: 978 0 19 404557 5
CLASS BOOK ISBN: 978 0 19 404558 2
LINGOKIDS A APP ISBN: 978 0 19 403495 1

Printed in China

This book is printed on paper from certified and well-managed sources

ACKNOWLEDGEMENTS

Back cover photograph: Oxford University Press building/David Fisher

Main character illustrations by: Emma McCann

Cover illustration by: Emma McCann

Illustrations by: Mike Byrne/Advocate pp.11, 13, Pop-Out Festivals - Christmas,
Pop-Out Festivals - Spring, Pop-Out Festivals - Summer, Stickers: Unit 3, Unit
6, Unit 9; Emma McCann pp.1, 4 (Tex), 7, 8, 10 (Tex), 12 (Frankie), 14 (Spot),
16 (Dizzy), 17, 18 (Tex), 19, 21, 22 (Spot), 24 (Tex), 26 (Frankie), 26 (Spot), 27,
28 (Frankie), 30 (Tex), 32 (Frankie), 33, 34 (Spot), 36 (Dizzy), 37 (Tex, Frankie,
Dizzy, Spot), 40 (Tex), 42 (Frankie), 44 (Tex), 46 (Frankie), 48 (Tex), 50 (Frankie)
Pop-Out Hello, Pop-Out Unit 1, Pop-Out Unit 2, Pop-Out Unit 3, Pop-Out Unit 4,
Pop-Out Unit 5, Stickers: Hello, Unit 1, Unit 2, Unit 3, Unit 4, Unit 5; Deborah
Van Der Leijgraaf/The Organisation pp.3, 5, 6, 9, 12, 14, 15, 19, 20, 23, 25, 29,
31, 35, 39, 41, 43, 45, 47, 49.

**The publishers advise that project work involving cutting and
sticking should be carried out under the supervision of an adult.**

Hello!

Hello, what's your name?

I'm Frankie!

I'm Tex!

I'm Dizzy!

I'm Spot!

Hello, what's your name?

Hello, what's your name? Hello, what's your name?
I'm Frankie, hello! I'm Frankie, hello!
Hi, how are you?
I'm fine, thank you!

Hello, what's your name? Hello, what's your name?
I'm Tex, hello! I'm Tex, hello!
Hi, how are you?
I'm fine, thank you!

Hello, what's your name? Hello, what's your name?
I'm Dizzy, hello! I'm Dizzy, hello!
Hi, how are you?
I'm fine, thank you!

Hello, what's your name? Hello, what's your name?
I'm Spot, hello! I'm Spot, hello!
Hi, how are you?
I'm fine, thank you!

Use the stickers.

unit 1 Look at my mask!

Tex's words

face

eyes

ears

nose

mouth

hair

Touch your face

Touch your face, 1, 2, 3.
Stand up. Touch your face.
Copy me!

Touch your eyes, 1, 2, 3.
Stand up. Touch your eyes.
Copy me!

Touch your ears, 1, 2, 3.
Stand up. Touch your ears.
Copy me!

Touch your nose, 1, 2, 3.
Stand up. Touch your nose.
Copy me!

Touch your mouth, 1, 2, 3.
Stand up. Touch your mouth.
Copy me!

Touch your hair, 1, 2, 3.
Stand up. Touch your hair.
Copy me!

Use the stickers.

4

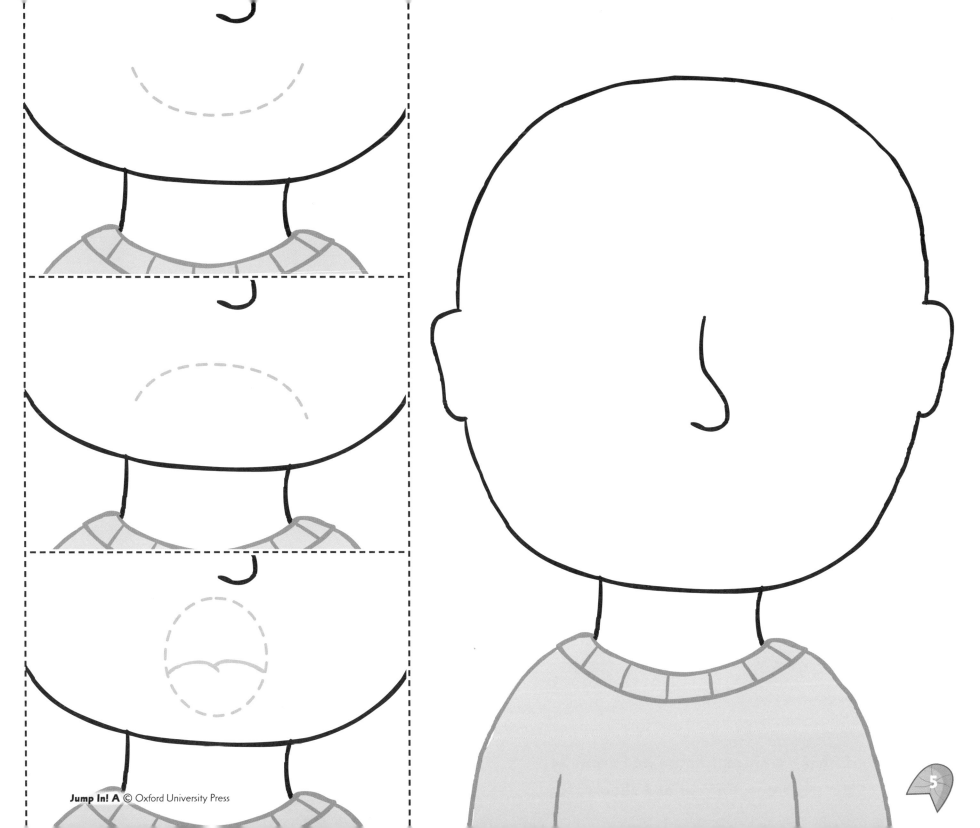

Frankie talks

How are you?
I'm happy.

How are you?
I'm sad.

How are you?
I'm sleepy.

Hello, how are you?

Hello, how are you? *(x2)*
I'm happy! And you?
I'm happy, too!

Hello, how are you? *(x2)*
I'm sad! And you?
I'm sad, too!

Hello, how are you? *(x2)*
I'm sleepy! And you?
I'm sleepy, too!

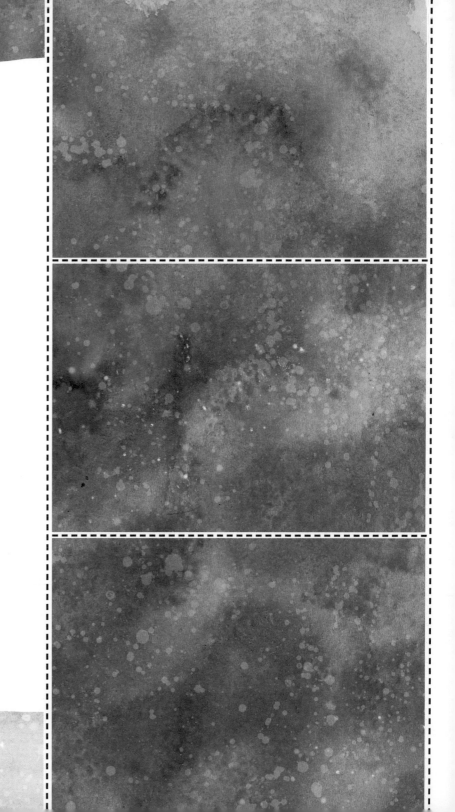

Either ▢ Trace. Choose and draw. Say.
or ✂ Trace. Cut out and choose. Say.

Tex's words

mummy

daddy

sister

brother

granny

grandad

We are a family

Families can be big.
Families can be small.
I love my family best of all.

I love my mummy.
My mummy loves me.
We are a family.

I love my daddy …

Families can be …

I love my sister …

I love my brother …

Families can be …

I love my granny …

I love my grandad …

Families can be …

Use the stickers. Colour.

11

Frankie talks

What's your favourite colour?

orange
brown
purple
pink

red
yellow
green
blue

What's your favourite colour?

What's your favourite colour? *(x3)*
Tell us please.

Is it orange? Is it brown? Is it purple or pink?
Everybody. Think! Think! Think!

Is it red? Is it yellow? Is it green or blue?
We like colours. How about you?

Look and colour. Say.
Make a 'favourite colour' poster. Draw and stick.

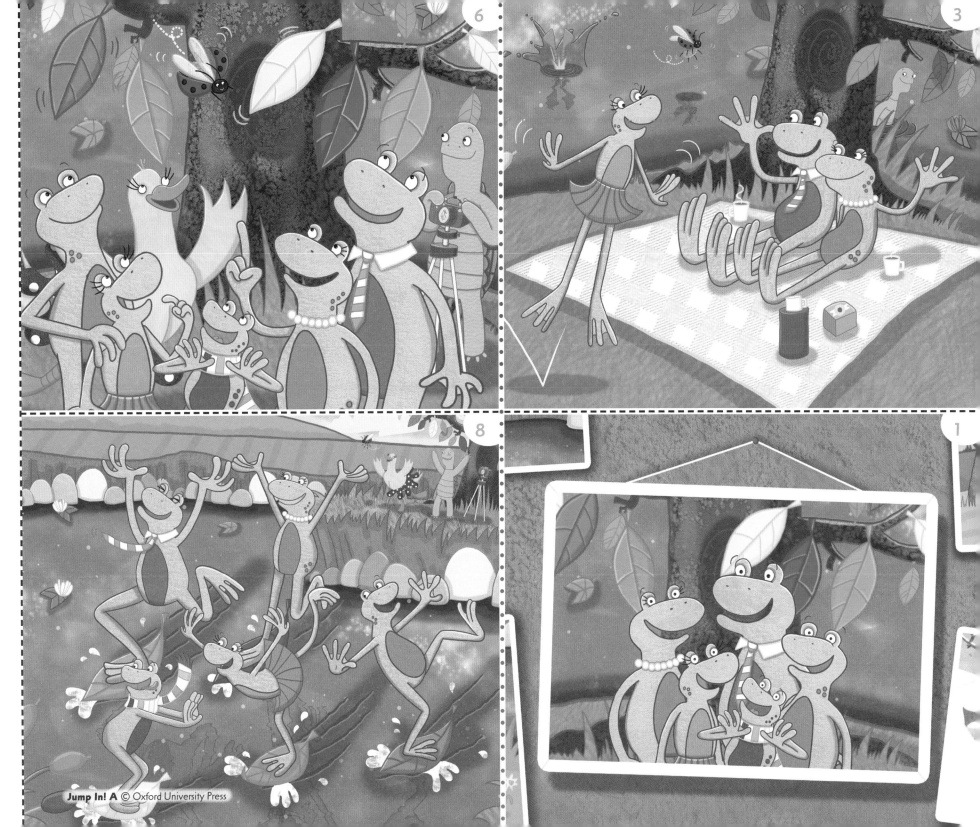

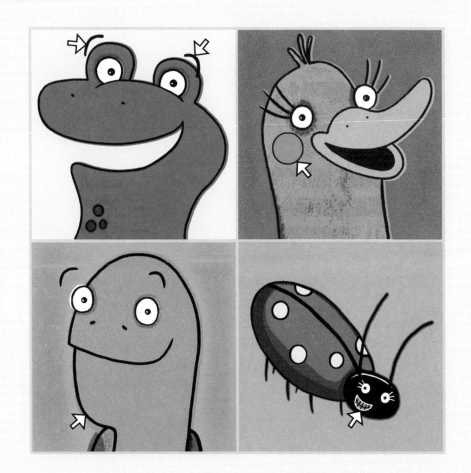

Dizzy's project

eyebrows

cheeks

chin

teeth

I can paint a face
Tune: Day-O

Painting, painting.
I like painting. Do you like it too?

Painting, painting.
I can paint a face. How about you?

Hair and eyes and eyebrows, too.
I can paint a face. How about you?

Ears and cheeks and chin, too.
I like painting. How about you?

Nose and mouth and teeth, too.
Now I've finished. How about you?

Sing. Make pop art versions of Frankie, Dizzy, Tex and Spot.

Tex's words

fire fighter

chef

shop assistant

teacher

doctor

waiter

Are you a ...?
Tune: Frère Jacques

Are you a fire fighter? *(x2)*
Yes I am. Yes I am.
I'm a fire fighter. I'm a fire fighter.
I help you. I help you.

Are you a chef? *(x2)*
Yes I am. Yes I am.
I'm a chef. I'm a chef.
I help you. I help you.

Are you a shop assistant? *(x2)*
Yes I am. Yes I am.
I'm a shop assistant. I'm a shop assistant.
I help you. I help you.

Are you a teacher? *(x2)*
Yes I am. Yes I am.
I'm a teacher. I'm a teacher.
I help you. I help you.

Are you a doctor? *(x2)*
Yes I am. Yes I am.
I'm a doctor. I'm a doctor.
I help you. I help you.

Are you a waiter? *(x2)*
Yes I am. Yes I am.
I'm a waiter. I'm a waiter.
I help you. I help you.

Use the stickers.

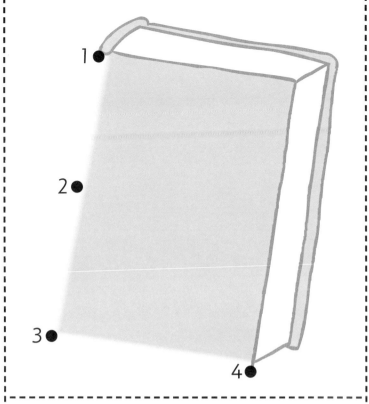

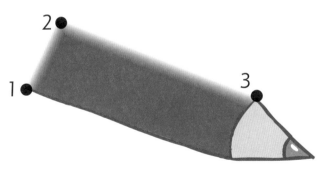

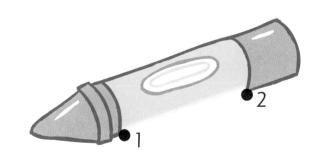

19

Frankie talks

Can I have a school bag / book /
pencil / crayon, please?
Here you are. Anything else?

Can I have a school bag?

Can I have a school bag, a school bag, a school bag?
Can I have a school bag, a school bag, please?
Yes, here you are.
Anything else, anything else, anything else?

Can I have a book ...?

Can I have a pencil ...?

Can I have a crayon ...?

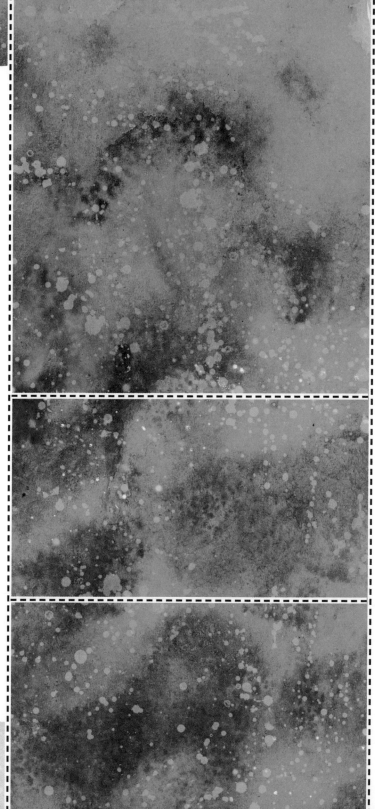

Either ⬜ **Join the dots and say.**
or ✂ **Join the dots. Cut out and say.**

unit 4 I'm hungry!

Tex's words

sandwiches

cheese

chicken

salad

spaghetti

chocolate

Do you like ...?

Tune: She'll be coming round the mountain

Do you like sandwiches?
Yes, I do.
Do you like sandwiches?
Yes, I do.
Do you like sandwiches? *(x3)*
Yes, I do.

Do you like cheese? ...

Do you like chicken? ...

Do you like salad? ...

Do you like spaghetti? ...

Do you like chocolate? ...

Use the stickers.

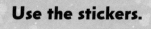

24

Frankie talks

I like juice / bananas / yoghurt.

I like spaghetti / sandwiches / salad.

I like cheese / chicken / chocolate.

I like ...

Juice, juice, I like juice.
Bananas, bananas, I like bananas.
Yoghurt, yoghurt, I like yoghurt, too.

Spaghetti, spaghetti, I like spaghetti.
Sandwiches, sandwiches, I like sandwiches.
Salad, salad, I like salad, too.

Cheese, cheese, I like cheese.
Chicken, chicken, I like chicken.
Chocolate, chocolate, I like chocolate, too.

What do you like? Draw a 🙂 or 🙁. Say.

Wake up, Tex!

Tex's words

cow

horse

pig

sheep

hen

chick

Down on the farm

Tune: The wheels on the bus

The cow on the farm goes moo, moo, moo.
Moo, moo, moo. *(x2)*
The cow on the farm goes moo, moo, moo.
Down on the farm.

The horse on the farm goes neigh, neigh, neigh …

The pig on the farm goes oink, oink, oink …

The sheep on the farm goes baa, baa, baa …

The hen on the farm goes cluck, cluck, cluck …

The chick on the farm goes cheep, cheep, cheep …

Use the stickers.

Frankie talks

Good morning!
It's time to get out of bed.
Open your eyes.

Goodnight!
It's time to go to bed.
Close your eyes.

Good morning, sun!

Tune: My bonnie lies over the ocean

Good morning, Good morning, sun!
It's time to get out of bed.
Open your little eyes.
Lift your sleepy head.

Good morning, sun!
Good morning, sun!
It's time to get out of bed, bed, bed.
Good morning, sun!
Good morning, sun!
It's time to get out of bed.

Goodnight, Goodnight, moon!
It's time to go to bed.
Close your little eyes.
Lay down your sleepy head.

Goodnight, moon!
Goodnight, moon!
It's time to go to bed, bed, bed.
Goodnight, moon!
Goodnight, moon!
It's time to go to bed.

Either 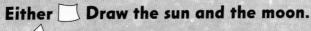 **Draw the sun and the moon.**
or 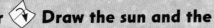 **Draw the sun and the moon. Fold and stick. Play.**

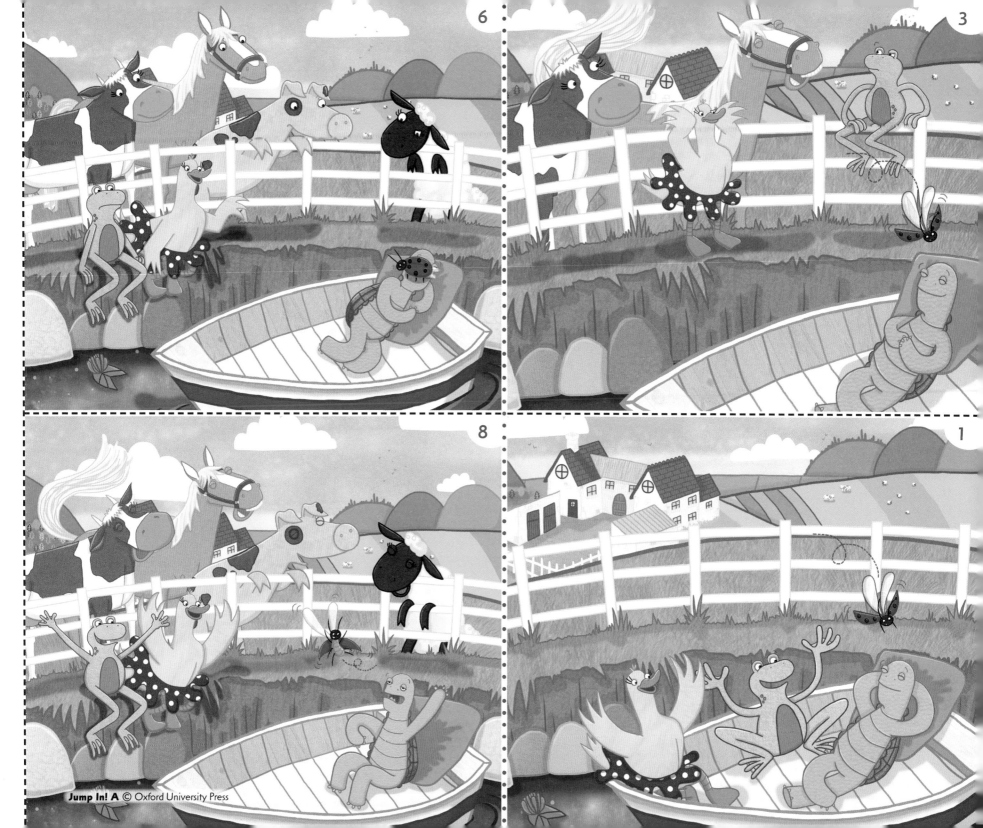

3

2

4

1

35

Project 2

Dizzy's project

egg

shell

wing

beak

Cluck, cluck, cluck

Cluck, cluck, cluck
Goes the big red hen.
Then she lays
A warm, brown egg.

Peck, peck, peck
On the shell of the egg.
Out comes a wing
Out comes a leg.

Crack, crack, crack
Out comes the chick.
Mummy, Mummy
Come here quick.

The little chick
Goes cheep, cheep, cheep.
And peck, peck, peck
With her little beak.

 36

Either ☐ **Sing. Trace and colour the egg brown.**

or ✄ **Sing. Trace and colour the egg brown. Fold and play.**

Jump In!

Extra Activities

Tex's words

computer game

puppet

train

book

car

costume

Can you see?

Tune: Here we go Looby Loo

Can you see a computer game? *(x3)*
Everyone point with me.

Can you see a puppet? *(x3)*
Everyone point with me.

Can you see a train? *(x3)*
Everyone point with me.

Can you see a book? *(x3)*
Everyone point with me.

Can you see a car? *(x3)*
Everyone point with me.

Can you see a costume? *(x3)*
Everyone point with me.

Use the stickers.

Frankie talks

What do you want for Christmas?

*I want a computer game / puppet /
train / book / car / costume, please.*

What do you want for Christmas?

What do you want for Christmas? *(x3)*
Tell us, please.

I want a computer game. *(x3)*
I want a computer game, please.

I want a puppet. *(x3)*
I want a puppet, please.

I want a train. *(x3)*
I want a train, please.

I want a book. *(x3)*
I want a book, please.

I want a car. *(x3)*
I want a car, please.

I want a costume. *(x3)*
I want a costume, please.

Circle what you want for Christmas. Say.

Festivals Spring

Tex's words

seeds

shoots

stems

leaves

buds

flowers

Early in spring

Tune: Here we go round the mulberry bush

This is the way we plant the seeds,
Plant the seeds, plant the seeds.
This is the way we plant the seeds,
Early in spring.

This is the way we water the seeds …

This is the way the shoots grow …

This is the way the stems grow …

This is the way the leaves grow …

This is the way the buds grow …

This is the way the flowers grow …

Use the stickers.

Frankie talks

Look on the flowers.

Look under the leaves.

Look in the pond.

Easter Bunny

Tune: In and out those dusty bluebells

Here comes the Easter Bunny. *(x3)*
Hiding chocolate eggs.

Look on the flowers. Where can the eggs be?
Look under the leaves. Where can the eggs be?
Look in the pond. Where can the eggs be?
How many can you see?

Hunting for eggs. Put them in my basket. *(x3)*
Now my basket's full.

Find the eggs. Look and count.

Festivals Summer

Tex's words

sun cream

sun hat

T-shirt

water

sun umbrella

sunglasses

Safe in the sun

Tune: What shall we do with the drunken sailor?

Wear sun cream, everyone. *(x3)*
Be safe in the sun.

Wear a sun hat, everyone. *(x3)*
Be safe in the sun.

Wear a T-shirt, everyone. *(x3)*
Be safe in the sun.

Drink water, everyone. *(x3)*
Be safe in the sun.

Use a sun umbrella, everyone. *(x3)*
Be safe in the sun.

Wear sunglasses, everyone. *(x3)*
Be safe in the sun.

Use the stickers.

Frankie talks

Let's have a picnic!

oranges

apples

cherries

Let's have a picnic!

Tune: Pop! Goes the weasel

Sandwiches, salad, chicken and cheese.
Oranges, apples and cherries.
Chocolate, yoghurt, water and juice!
Let's have a picnic!

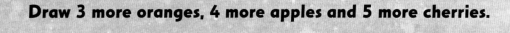

Draw 3 more oranges, 4 more apples and 5 more cherries.

Make a funny faces book.

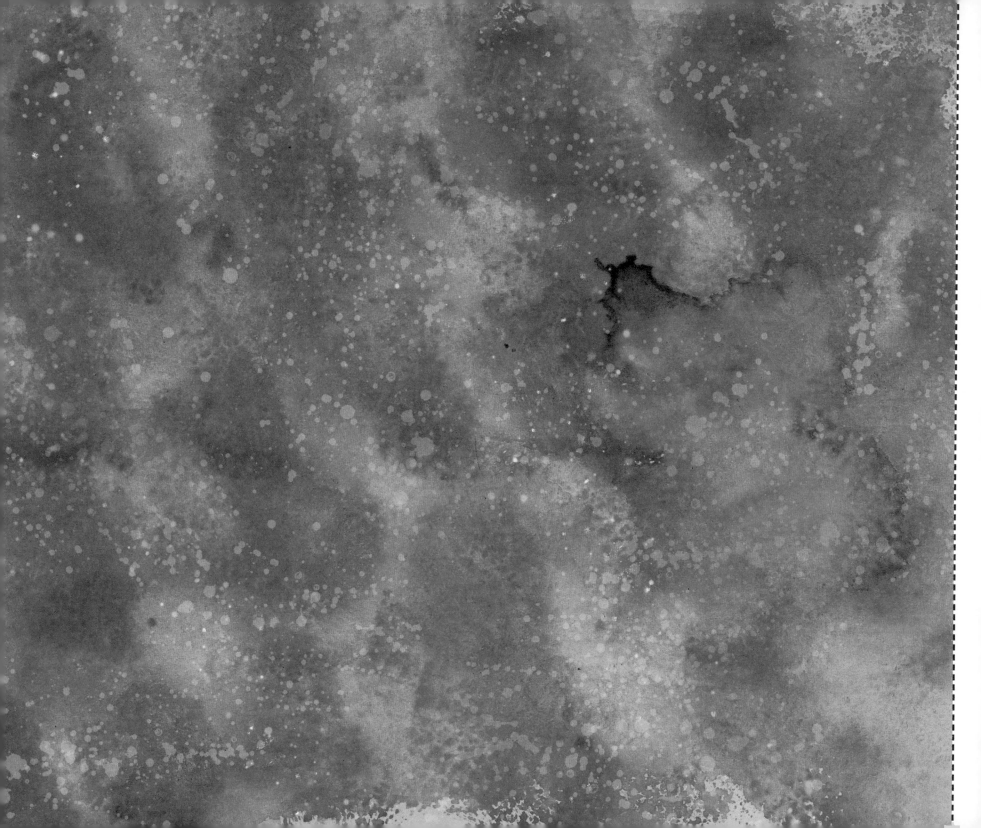

Make a funny faces book.

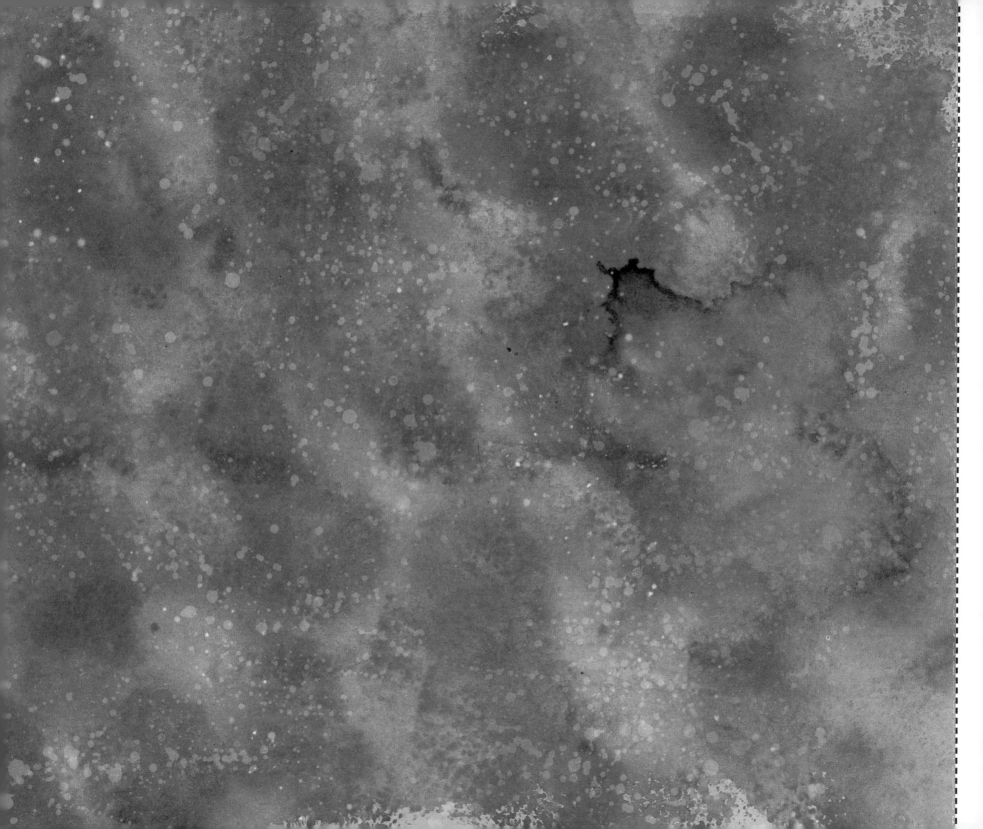

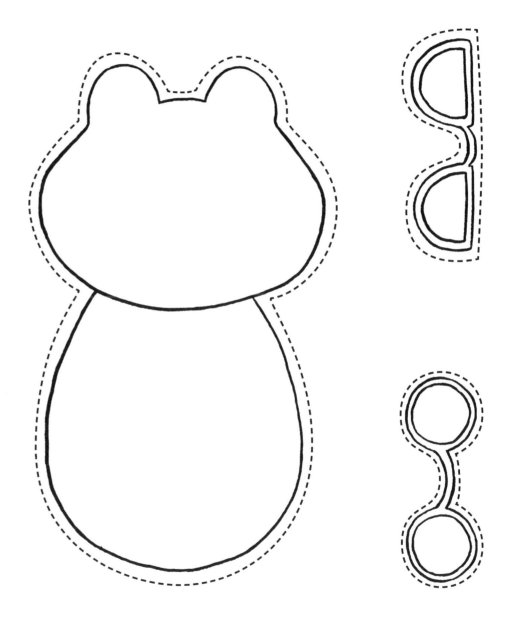

Make the frog family.

55

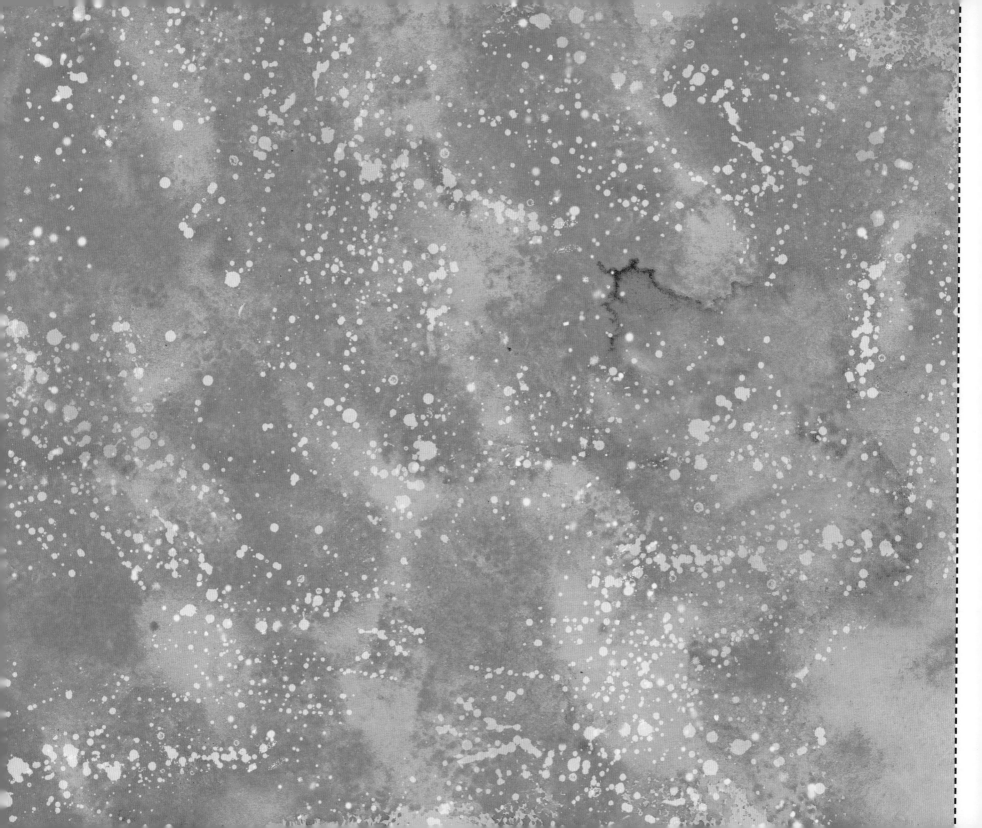

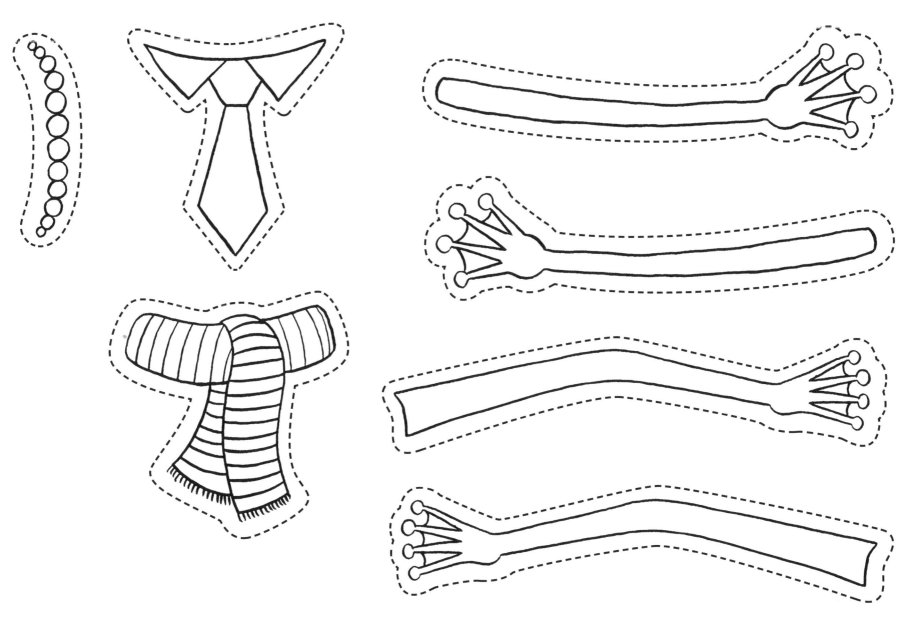

Make the frog family.

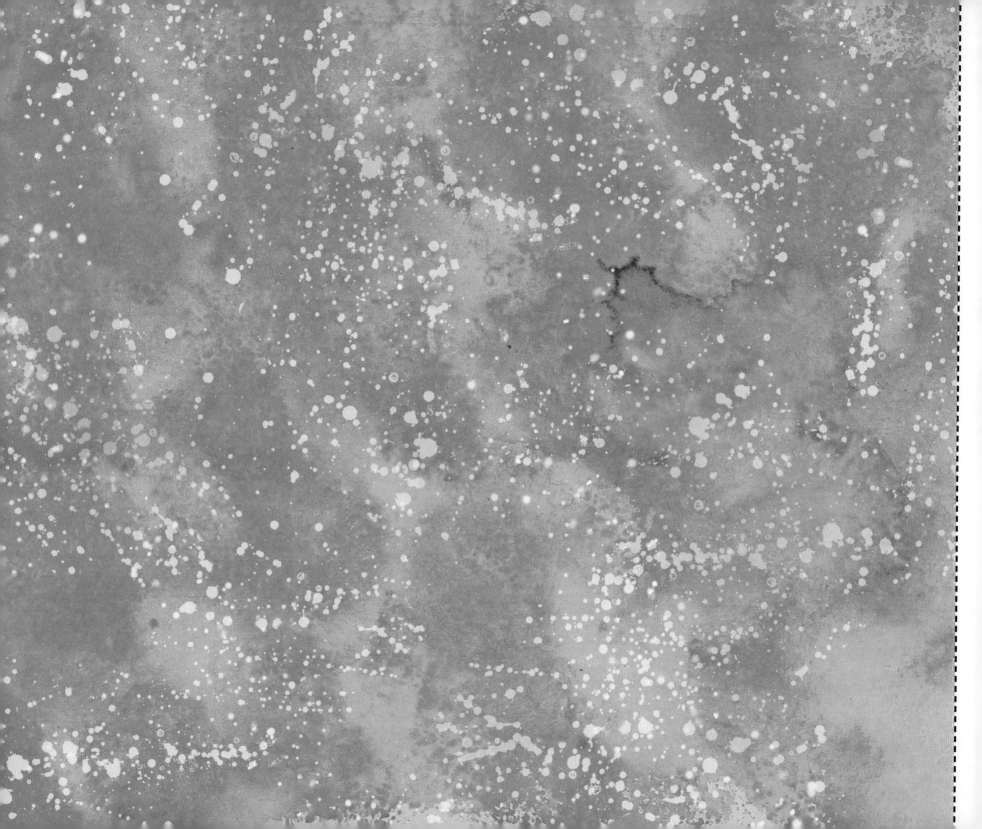

Match the jobs.

Match the foods.

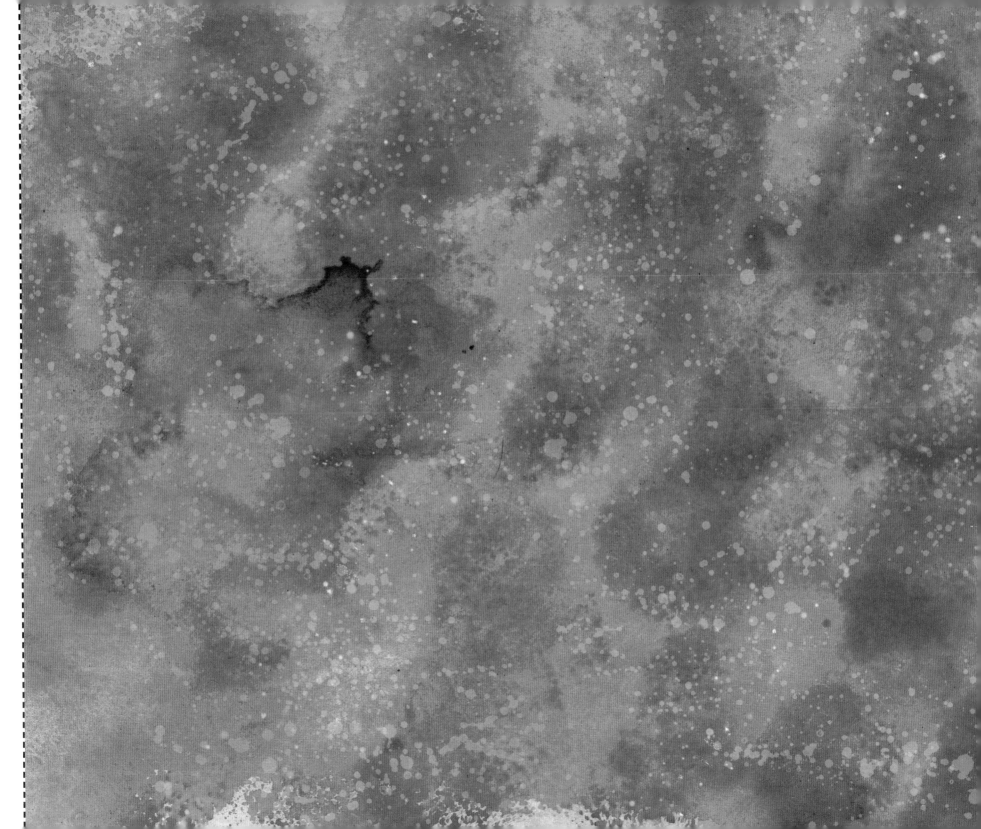

Play the farm game.